For Mum, with love

~ J.B.

To Isabella, with much love

~ R.B.

Text copyright © 2008 Janet Bingham
Illustrations copyright © 2008 Rosalind Beardshaw

Library of Congress Cataloging-in-Publication Data

Bingham, Janet, 1959-
[New home for Little Fox]
Daddy's little scout / written by Janet Bingham ; illustrated by Rosalind Beardshaw.
   p. cm.
 Summary: Previously published: London : Scholastic Children's Books,
2008 under the title, A new home for Little Fox.
 Summary: Little Fox and his father look at other woodland animals'
homes, then make a new den for themselves.
 ISBN-13: 978-0-545-16496-2 (alk. paper)
 ISBN-10: 0-545-16496-6 (alk. paper)
 [1. Animals--Habitations--Fiction. 2. Fathers and sons--Fiction. 3.
Foxes--Fiction.] I. Beardshaw, Rosalind, ill. II. Title.

PZ7.B5118168Dad 2010
[E]--dc22   2009009619

ISBN: 978-0-545-16496-2

10 9 8 7 6 5 4 3 2 1   10 11 12 13 14/0

Printed in Singapore • First Scholastic US printing, January 2010

Daddy's Little Scout

Written by
Janet Bingham

Illustrated by
Rosalind Beardshaw

Cartwheel
·B·O·O·K·S·®

SCHOLASTIC INC.
New York   Toronto   London   Auckland
Sydney   Mexico City   New Delhi   Hong Kong

Little Fox was making music.

"La, la, la!" he sang.

"Shhh!" said Daddy Fox. "Listen!"
Little Fox stopped singing.

"Tweet-tweet-tweet," sang the tree, sweetly.

"What's that?" asked Little Fox.
"Is the tree making music, too?"
"It's Mrs. Finch," replied
Daddy Fox. "She's singing
her nest-building song."

"Can I see?" asked Little Fox.

Daddy Fox lifted him up higher and higher
until he could see the little twiggy nest.

Just then a nut landed—clonk—
on Little Fox's head.
   "Whoops!" chuckled Daddy Fox.
"That's the trouble with trees—
things drop out of them."
   "It's Squirrel!" said Little Fox.
"Is she building a nest, too?"

"She's spring-cleaning," said Daddy Fox. "Everyone starts thinking about their nests and dens in the spring. They make new ones, or tidy up their old ones…"

"We can make a new home, too!" burst out Little Fox.

"Let's build a nest high up in the tree!"

"Trees are too high for us," smiled Daddy Fox. "They wobble and sway in the wind. We might fall out of them, like nuts!"

"I don't want to fall like a nut, but it's fun to roll like one," giggled Little Fox.

And away they tumbled...

...straight into a bush.

"Ooof!" groaned Daddy Fox.
"I'm seeing stars."
"They're not stars, they're butterflies!"
laughed Little Fox.

"Let's make our new home here, in
the butterfly-flowers!"

He leaned over to smell the blossoms, and yelped,
"Ouch! Prickles!"
Daddy Fox hugged him. "It wouldn't be very
comfortable to live here," he said.

Little Fox scampered ahead.

"Look, Daddy, I've found a mouse's house," he whispered. "Perhaps we could live down here."

"We're too big and noisy," Daddy Fox whispered back. "We'd spoil poor Mouse's hideaway."

But Little Fox wasn't listening. A dragonfly skimmed past his nose, and he was off . . .

… chasing and racing over the soft grass, until Daddy Fox caught up with him at the stream. "This is where the fish live," said Daddy Fox. Little Fox dabbled at the water. "I'm glad I don't live in here," he said. "It's wet and cold and runny."

"Like your nose!" teased Daddy Fox.
Little Fox splashed him. "Like **your** nose!"
He giggled, running back up the bank.

All of a sudden, a dome of crumbly earth popped up, with a little pink nose poking out of the top.

"What is it?" asked Little Fox.
"It's Mr. Mole," said Daddy Fox.
"He's tidying his tunnels."

Mr. Mole's nose disappeared back into the molehill.
"I wouldn't want to live down there," said Little Fox.
"It's **too dark** for me!"
And off he ran to the meadow.

"Look!" said Daddy Fox. "Rabbit holes and lots of rabbits."

"One, two, three ..."
counted Little Fox. "I can see ten!"

"It must be very crowded in their house,"
said Daddy Fox. "Come on, it's time to go!"
And they raced away toward home.

Little Fox peered into their den.
"Our home might get crowded, too,"
he frowned. "It looks very small."
"That's because you have grown so
big," laughed Daddy Fox. "It's time
for us to move to a new home now."

And that's just what they did.
They dug and dug all afternoon …

... until at last they were finished.

"I'm glad our new home isn't high in a tree or in a prickly bush," said Little Fox, "or in a cold wet stream or a mouse's house or a dark molehill ..."

"Or in a busy rabbit warren," smiled Daddy Fox.

That night, Little Fox peeped out
of their newly dug den.
"This home is just right," he sighed happily.
"Yes," agreed Daddy Fox, hugging him close.

"It's the best home of all...

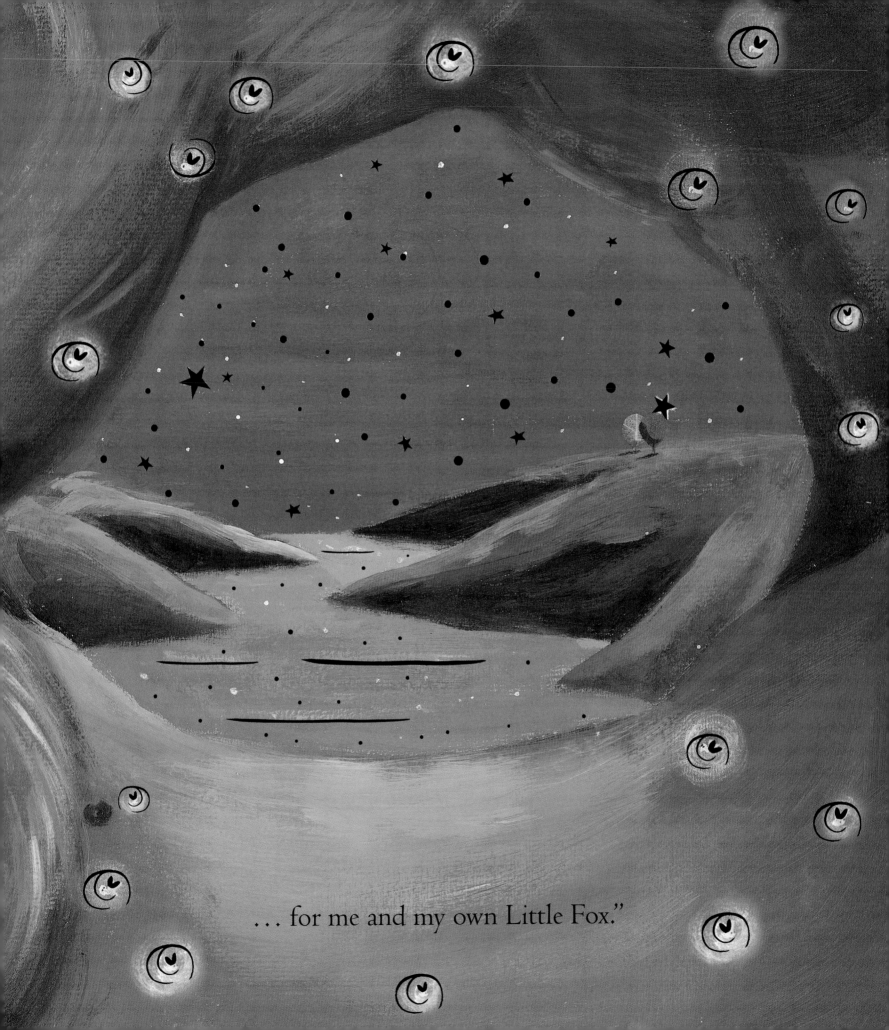

...for me and my own Little Fox."

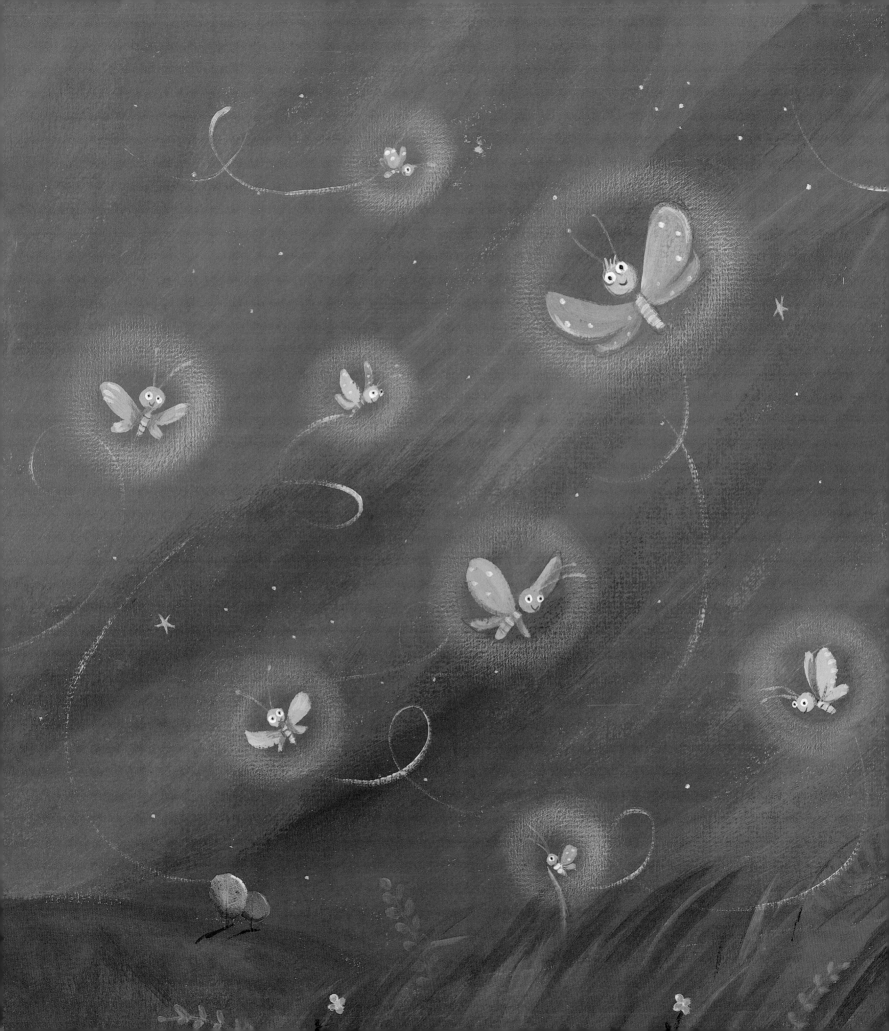